MW00508735

Comfort Food Recipes

A Quickstart Guide To Quick And Easy Comfort Food For Everyday Meal Ideas For Breakfast, Lunch And Dinner With Over Great Tasting

Erin Wilkinson

Table of Contents

Introduction

If you're picking up this book, you may have been missing out on comfort foods for some time now. I'm happy to say that those times are about to come to an end. You no longer need to give up fluffy dinner rolls, macaroni, and cheese, or your mother's hearty casserole. I'll show you how to put them back on the dinner table.

We all love and care about our favorite comfort foods. They are the foods that replace a warm hug from grandmother. They are our go-to foods on cold winter days, after breakups, and after a bad day. They remind us of our childhood days; they remind us of meals shared with our best friends, crushes, and soul mates.

Packed with vibrant flavors and regional inspirations, this book provides you with an exclusive collection of over 600 international comfort foods. Indulge yourself in the wealth of international comfort foods to explore your new favorites.

It's time to comfort yourself with a hot soothing bowl of your favorite dish and indulge in its delightful flavors. Get ready to curl up in the company of these delicious comfort foods.

The Nostalgia of Comfort Foods

The concept of comforting home cooking is growing rapidly among food enthusiasts. Comfort foods can be prepared in any season. Just one bowl of these around-the-globe comfort foods can bring a smile to your face when you need it most. Ever wondered why our favorite comfort foods taste so great? It has a psychological connection to it. When you prepare your favorite comfort food, it emits its unique aroma. That aroma enters your nasal cavity and reaches your limbic system, which is associated with long-term memory and emotions. When this system senses a familiar aroma, it recognizes its earlier interactions, which triggers pleasure. That is why we crave and love our favorite comfort foods. You do not need an excuse to make them; they are simple and yet never fail to give their warm love. Their soothing aroma is enough to bring everyone together at the dining table.

Comfort food is amazing. What else can evoke childhood memories of family, soothe that homesick feeling, and stitch together a broken heart?

Rainy days are suddenly sunny when you are homebound with the aroma of your mother's pot pie. Sore throats are soothed slurping down a steaming bowl of chicken noodle soup. A stressful day at work fades after you devour a slice of chocolate cake.

Why? Because our senses bring back memories—smells, tastes, textures—that comfort foods radiate straight to our hearts. We are instantly transported. How do you feel thinking about gooey cheese stretching from slices of lasagna, warm spaghetti noodles twirling on grandma's antique fork or that first bite of fluffy pancakes on Sunday morning?

Chapter 1: Breakfast Recipes

1. Mini Veggie Quiche

Preparation Time: 10 minutes | Cooking Time: 20 minutes | Servings: 12

Ingredients:

6 eggs

1/4 cup bell pepper, diced

3/4 cup cheddar cheese, shredded

10 oz frozen spinach, chopped

1/4 cup onion, chopped

1/4 cup mushroom, diced

Directions:

Add all ingredients into the large bowl and whisk until combined.

Pour egg mixture into the 12 silicone muffin molds.

Place the dehydrating tray in a multi-level air fryer basket and place basket in the instant pot.

Place 6 muffin molds on a dehydrating tray.

Seal pot with air fryer lid and select bake mode then set

the temperature to 350 F and timer for 20 minutes.

Bake remaining muffins using the same method.

Serve and enjoy.

Nutrition:

Calories 67, Fat 4.6 g, Carbohydrates 1.6 g, Sugar 0.6 g,

Protein 5.3 g, Cholesterol 89 mg

2. Broccoli Cheese Loaf

Preparation Time: 10 minutes | Cooking Time: 30 minutes | Servings: 4

Ingredients:

5 eggs, lightly beaten

3/4 cup broccoli florets, chopped

1 cup cheddar cheese, shredded

2 tsp baking powder

3 1/1 tbsp coconut flour

1 tsp salt

Directions:

Spray a loaf pan with cooking spray and set aside.

Add all ingredients into the bowl and mix well.

Pour egg mixture into the prepared loaf pan.

Place steam rack into the instant pot then places loaf

pan on top of the rack.

Seal pot with air fryer lid and select bake mode then set

the temperature to 350 F and timer for 30 minutes.

Serve and enjoy.

Nutrition:

Calories 231, Fat 15.7 g, Carbohydrates 8.1 g, Sugar 0.9

g, Protein 15.4 g, Cholesterol 234 mg

3. Chicken Casserole

Preparation Time: 10 minutes | Cooking Time: 25 minutes | Servings: 8

Ingredients:

2 lbs cooked chicken, shredded

6 oz cream cheese, softened

4 oz butter, melted

6 oz ham, cut into small pieces

5 oz Swiss cheese 1 oz fresh lemon juice

1 tbsp Dijon mustard 1/2 tsp salt

Directions:

Spray instant pot from inside with cooking spray.

Add chicken and ham into the instant pot and spread evenly.

Add butter, lemon juice, mustard, cream cheese, and salt into the blender and blend until a thick sauce.

Spread sauce over top of chicken and ham mixture.

Arrange Swiss cheese slices on top of the sauce.

Seal pot with air fryer lid and select bake mode then set the temperature to 350 F and timer for 25 minutes.

Serve and enjoy.

Nutrition:

Calories 451, Fat 29.2 g, Carbohydrates 2.5 g, Sugar 0.4 g, Protein 43g, Cholesterol 170 mg.

4. Baked Chicken & Mushrooms

Preparation Time: 10 minutes | Cooking Time: 30 minutes | Servings: 2

Ingredients:

2 chicken breasts, boneless and skinless

1/4 cup sun-dried tomatoes

4 oz mushrooms, sliced

1/4 cup mayonnaise

1/2 tsp salt

Directions:

Line instant pot multi-level air fryer basket with foil.

Brush chicken breast with mayonnaise and place it into the air fryer basket and place the basket into the instant pot.

Add sun-dried tomatoes, mushrooms, and salt on top of the chicken.

Seal pot with air fryer lid and select bake mode then set the temperature to 380 F and timer for 30 minutes.

Serve and enjoy.

Nutrition:

Calories 408, Fat 20.8 g, Carbohydrates 9.8 g, Sugar 3.4 g, Protein 44.5 g, Cholesterol 138 mg.

5. Bacon Egg Muffins

Preparation Time: 10 minutes | Cooking Time: 25 minutes | Servings: 12

Ingredients:

12 eggs 8 bacon slices, cooked and crumbled

2 tbsp fresh parsley, chopped 1/2 tsp mustard powder

1/3 cup heavy cream 2 green onion, chopped

4 oz cheddar cheese, shredded Pepper

Salt

Directions:

In a mixing bowl, whisk together eggs, mustard powder, heavy cream, pepper, and salt.

Divide cheddar cheese, onions, and bacon into the 12 silicone muffin molds.

Pour egg mixture into the muffin molds.

Place the dehydrating tray in a multi-level air fryer basket and place basket in the instant pot.

Place 6 muffin molds on a dehydrating tray.

Seal pot with air fryer lid and select bake mode then set the temperature to 375 F and timer for 25 minutes.

Serve and enjoy.

Nutrition:

Calories 183, Fat 14.1 g, Carbohydrates 1 g, Sugar 0.5 g, Protein 12.8 g, Cholesterol 192 mg.

6. Sweet Squash Breakfast

Preparation time: 10 minutes | Cooking Time: 4 minutes | Servings: 4

Ingredients:

1 ½ cups coconut milk, unsweetened

A pinch of ground cloves

A pinch of ground nutmeg

1 small zucchini, grated

5 oz squash, grated

2 tablespoons swerve

½ teaspoon ground cinnamon

¼ cup chopped pecans

Directions:

In your instant pot, mix milk with cloves, nutmeg, zucchini, squash, swerve, cinnamon and pecans. Stir, cover, and cook on High pressure for 4 minutes.

Divide into bowls and serve hot.

Enjoy!

Nutrition:

Calories 100, fat 1g, fiber 2g, carbs 3g, Protein 4g.

7. Okra and Zucchini Breakfast

Preparation time: 10 minutes | Cooking Time: 10 minutes | Servings: 4

Ingredients:

1 ½ cups chopped red onion

3 tablespoons olive oil

2 cups sliced okra

1 cup sliced mushrooms

1 cup cherry tomatoes, halved

1 cup of water

2 cups chopped zucchini

2 cups chopped yellow bell pepper

Black pepper to the taste

2 tablespoons chopped basil

1 tablespoon chopped thyme

½ cup balsamic vinegar

Directions:

Put onion, tomato, okra, mushrooms, zucchini, bell pepper, basil, thyme, vinegar, and oil in your instant pot and toss.

Add black pepper, toss again then add the water. Cover pot and cook on High pressure for 10 minutes.

Divide between plates and serve for breakfast.

Enjoy!

Nutrition:

Calories 120, fat 2g, fiber 2g, carbs 3g, Protein 6g.

8. Pumpkin Oatmeal

Preparation Time: 10 minutes | Cooking Time: 10 minutes | Servings: 4

Ingredients:

1 cup steel-cut oats

2 tbsp maple syrup

1/4 cup pumpkin

1/4 tsp cinnamon

1 tbsp brown sugar

1 tsp vanilla

1 1/4 cups water

14 oz can coconut milk

1/2 tsp salt

Directions:

Add oats, vanilla, water, coconut milk, and salt into the instant pot and stir well.

Seal pot with the lid and select manual high pressure for 10 minutes.

Release pressure using the quick-release method than open the lid.

Stir in cinnamon, brown sugar, maple syrup, and pumpkin.

Serve and enjoy.

Nutrition:

Calorie 187, Carbohydrates 25.9g, Protein 4.5g, Fat 7.2g, Sugar 10.6g, Sodium 303mg.

Chapter 2: Lunch Recipes

9. Fennel Chicken

Preparation Time: 10 minutes | Cooking Time: 15 minutes | Servings: 4

Ingredients:

1 lb chicken thighs, boneless and cut into three pieces

1 tsp cayenne

1 tsp turmeric

1 tsp garam masala

1 tsp ground fennel seeds

1 tsp paprika

2 tsp garlic, minced

2 tsp ginger, minced

1 tbsp olive oil

1 onion, sliced Pepper Salt

Directions:

Add chicken and remaining ingredients into the mixing

bowl and toss well and place it in the refrigerator

overnight.

Spray instant pot multi-level air fryer basket with cooking spray.

Add marinated chicken mixture into the air fryer basket and place basket into the instant pot.

Seal pot with air fryer lid and select air fry mode then set the temperature to 360°F and timer for 15 minutes.

Mix halfway through.

Serve and enjoy.

Nutrition:

Calories 281, Fat 14.2g, Carbohydrates 0.7g, Sugar 0g, Protein 33g, Cholesterol 116mg.

10. Beef Pot Roast

Preparation time: 10 minutes | Cooking Time: 1 hour |

Servings: 6

Ingredients:

3 pounds beef roast

Salt and ground black pepper, to taste

17 ounces beef stock

3 ounces red wine

½ teaspoon chicken salt

½ teaspoon smoked paprika

1 yellow onion, peeled and chopped

4 garlic cloves, peeled and minced

3 carrots, peeled and chopped

5 potatoes, chopped

Directions:

In a bowl, mix the salt, pepper, chicken, salt, and paprika

and stir.

Rub the beef with this mixture and put it into the Instant

Pot.

Add the onion, garlic, stock, and wine, toss to coat, cover

the Instant Pot and cook on Meat Stew for 50 minutes.

Release the pressure, uncover the Instant Pot, add the

carrots and potatoes, cover again, and cook on the

Steam setting for 10 minutes.

Release the pressure again, uncover the Instant Pot, transfer the roast to a platter, drizzle cooking juices all over, and serve with the vegetables on the side.

Nutrition:

Calories 290, Fat 20g, Fiber 0g, Carbs 2g, Protein 25g.

11.   Beef and Vegetables

Preparation time: 10 minutes | Cooking Time: 30 minutes | Servings: 4

Ingredients:

2 tablespoons extra virgin olive oil

1½ pounds, beef chuck roast, cubed

4 tablespoons flour

1 yellow onion, peeled and chopped

2 tablespoons red wine

2 garlic cloves, peeled and minced

2 cups of water

2 cups beef stock

Salt and ground black pepper, to taste

1 bay leaf

½ teaspoon dried thyme

2 celery stalks, chopped

2 carrots, peeled and chopped

4 potatoes, chopped

½ bunch parsley, chopped

Directions:

Season the beef with salt and pepper and mix with half of the flour.

Set the Instant Pot on Sauté mode, add the oil and heat it.

Add the beef, brown for 2 minutes, and transfer to a bowl.

Add the onion to the Instant Pot, stir, and cook for 3 minutes.

Add the garlic, stir, and cook for 1 minute.

Add the wine, stir well, and cook for 15 seconds. Add the rest of the flour and stir well for 2 minutes.

Return the meat to the Instant Pot, add the stock, water, bay leaf, and thyme, stir, cover, and cook on the Meat/Stew setting for 12 minutes.

Release the pressure, uncover the Instant Pot, add the carrots, celery, and potatoes, stir, cover the Instant Pot, and cook on the Steam setting for 5 minutes.

Release the pressure naturally for 10 minutes, uncover

the Instant Pot, divide among plates, and serve with

parsley sprinkled on top.

Nutrition:

Calories 221, Fat 5.3g, Fiber 1g, Carbs 20.2g, Protein:

22.7g.

12.   Trout and Eggplant Mix

Preparation time: 10 minutes | Cooking Time: 15 minutes | Servings: 4

Ingredients:

4 trout fillets, boneless

2 scallions, chopped

2 eggplants, cubed

½ cup chicken stock

2 tablespoons parsley, chopped

3 tablespoons olive oil

A pinch of salt and black pepper

2 tablespoons smoked paprika

Directions:

Set the instant pot on Sauté mode, add the oil, heat it, add the scallions and the eggplant and cook for 2 minutes,

Add the rest of the ingredients except the parsley, put the lid on, and cook on High for 13 minutes.

Release the pressure naturally for 10 minutes, divide the mix between plates and serve with the parsley sprinkled on top.

Nutrition:

Calories 291, fat 16.8g, fiber 4.5g, carbs 6.4g, protein 20g.

13.   Salmon and Tomato Passata

Preparation time: 10 minutes | Cooking Time: 15 minutes | Servings: 4

Ingredients:

1 tablespoon olive oil

4 salmon fillets, boneless, skinless, and cubed

1 tablespoon rosemary, chopped

1 shallot, chopped

1 cup tomato passata

1 teaspoon chili powder

1 tablespoon chives, chopped

A pinch of salt and black pepper

Directions:

Set the instant pot on Sauté mode, add the oil, heat it, add the shallot and sauté for 2 minutes.

Add the rest of the ingredients, put the lid on, and cook on High for 12 minutes.

Release the pressure naturally for 10 minutes, divide the mix between plates and serve.

Nutrition:

Calories 291, fat 16.8g, fiber 4.5g, carbs 7.4g, protein 20g.

14. Salmon and Artichokes

Preparation time: 10 minutes | Cooking Time: 15 minutes | Servings: 4

Ingredients:

1 pound salmon, skinless, boneless, and cubed

2 spring onions, chopped

12 ounces canned artichokes, roughly chopped

1 and ½ cups chicken stock

A pinch of salt and black pepper

1 tablespoon cilantro, chopped

Directions:

In your instant pot, combine all the ingredients, put the

lid on, and cook on High for 15 minutes.

Release the pressure naturally for 10 minutes, divide everything between plates and serve.

Nutrition:

Calories 193, fat 7.1g, fiber 4.1g, carbs 6.4g, protein 24.5g.

15.   Trout and Spinach Mix

Preparation time: 5 minutes | Cooking Time: 15 minutes | Servings: 4

Ingredients:

6 trout fillets, boneless

2 tablespoons avocado oil

2 scallions, minced

2 garlic cloves, minced

2 tablespoons cilantro, chopped

1 cup baby spinach

A pinch of salt and black pepper

2 tablespoons balsamic vinegar

Directions:

Set the instant pot on Sauté mode, add the oil, heat it,

add the scallions and the garlic and sauté for 2 minutes.

Add the rest of the ingredients, put the lid on, and cook

on High for 12 minutes.

Release the pressure fast for 5 minutes, divide the mix

between plates and serve.

Nutrition:

Calories 194, fat 8.8g, fiber 0.7g, carbs 1.8g, protein

25.4g.

16. Sea Bass and Sauce

Preparation time: 10 minutes | Cooking Time: 15 minutes | Servings: 4

Ingredients:

4 sea bass fillets, boneless and skinless

2 tablespoons lime juice

2 garlic cloves, minced

1 shallot, chopped

1 cup chicken stock 1 cup tomato passata

A pinch of salt and black pepper

Directions:

In your instant pot, combine the fish with the rest of the

ingredients, put the lid on, and cook on High for 15 minutes.

Release the pressure naturally for 10 minutes, divide the mix between plates and serve.

Nutrition:

Calories 154, fat 2.9g, fiber 1.3g, carbs 2.5g, protein 25g.

17. Sea Bass and Pesto

Preparation time: 5 minutes | Cooking Time: 12 minutes | Servings: 4

Ingredients:

4 sea bass fillets, skinless, boneless

2 tablespoons olive oil

2 tablespoons garlic, chopped

1 cup basil, chopped

2 tablespoons pine nuts

A pinch of salt and black pepper

1 cup tomato passata

1 tablespoon parsley, chopped

Directions:

In your blender, combine the oil with the garlic, basil, pine nuts, salt, and pepper and pulse well.

In your instant pot, combine the sea bass with the pesto, salt, pepper, tomato passata, and parsley, put the lid on, and cook on High for 12 minutes.

Release the pressure fast for 5 minutes, divide the mix between plates and serve.

Nutrition:

Calories 237, fat 12.7g, fiber 1.3g, carbs 5.5g, protein 25.8g.

18. Tuna and Mustard Greens

Preparation time: 10 minutes | Cooking Time: 10 minutes | Servings: 4

Ingredients:

2 cups mustard greens

1 tablespoon olive oil

1 cup tomato passata

1 shallot, chopped

1 tablespoon basil, chopped

A pinch of salt and black pepper

14 ounces tuna fillets, boneless, skinless, and cubed

Directions:

Set your instant pot on Sauté mode, add the oil, heat it, add the shallot and sauté for 2 minutes.

Add rest of the ingredients, put the lid on, and cook on High for 8 minutes.

Release the pressure naturally for 10 minutes, divide the mix between plates and serve.

Nutrition:

Calories 124, fat 3.7g, fiber 1.9g, carbs 2.6g, protein 1.6g.

19. Salmon and Salsa

Preparation time: 10 minutes | Cooking Time: 8 minutes | Servings: 4

Ingredients:

4 salmon fillets, boneless

½ cup veggie stock

1 cup black olives, pitted

1 cup tomatoes, cubed

1 tablespoon basil, chopped

1 tablespoon olive oil

1 tablespoon balsamic vinegar

A pinch of salt and black pepper

1 tablespoon chives, chopped

Directions:

In your instant pot, combine the fish with the stock, salt, and pepper put the lid on, and cook on High for 8 minutes.

Release the pressure naturally for 10 minutes and divide the salmon between plates.

In a bowl, mix the olives with the rest of the ingredients, toss, add next to the salmon and serve.

Nutrition:

Calories 313, fat 18.2g, fiber 1.7g, carbs 4g, protein 35.4g.

20. Moist Cinnamon Muffins

Preparation Time: 10 minutes | Cooking Time: 15 minutes | Servings: 6

Ingredients:

1/4 cup pumpkin puree

1/4 cup almond butter

1/4 cup coconut oil

1/2 tbsp cinnamon

1/2 tsp baking powder

1 scoop vanilla protein powder

1/4 cup almond flour

Directions:

In a large bowl, mix all dry ingredients.

Add wet ingredients into the dry ingredients and mix until combined.

Pour batter into silicone muffin molds and place into the air fryer basket. Place basket into the pot.

Seal the pot with an air fryer lid and select bake mode and cook at 350°F for 15 minutes.

Serve and enjoy.

Nutrition:

Calories 80, Fat 7.1g, Carbohydrates 1.6g, Sugar 0.4g, Protein 3.5g, Cholesterol 0mg.

21. Meatloaf

Preparation Time: 10 minutes | Cooking Time: 40 minutes | Servings: 8

Ingredients:

2 eggs 1/2 cup parmesan cheese, grated

1/2 cup marinara sauce, sugar-free

1 cup cottage cheese

1 lb mozzarella cheese, cut into cubes

2 lbs ground turkey 2 tsp Italian seasoning

1/4 cup basil pesto 1 tsp salt

Directions:

Grease instant pot loaf pan with butter and set aside.

Add all ingredients into the mixing bowl and mix until well combined.

Transfer bowl mixture into the prepared loaf pan.

Pour 1/2 cup water into the instant pot and place the steamer rack in the pot.

Place loaf pan on top of the steamer rack.

Seal the pot with an air fryer lid and select bake mode and cook at 400ºF for 40 minutes.

Slice and serve.

Nutrition:

Calories 350, Fat 18g, Carbohydrates 4.5g, Sugar 1g, Protein 42g, Cholesterol 177mg.

22. Bacon Egg Muffins

Preparation Time: 10 minutes | Cooking Time: 25 minutes | Servings: 6

Ingredients:

6 eggs 4 bacon slices, cooked and crumbled

1 tbsp fresh parsley, chopped

1/4 tsp mustard powder

1/4 cup heavy cream 2 tbsp green onion, chopped

2 oz cheddar cheee, shredded Pepper Salt

Directions:

In a bowl, whisk together eggs, mustard powder, heavy cream, pepper, and salt.

Divide cheddar cheese, onions, and bacon into the silicone muffin molds then pour egg mixture into each mold.

Place silicone muffin molds into the instant pot air fryer basket and place the basket in the pot.

Seal the pot with an air fryer lid and select bake mode and cook at 375ºF for 25 minutes.

Serve and enjoy.

Nutrition:

Calories 116, Fat 8g, Carbohydrates 1g, Sugar 0.5g, Protein 8sg, Cholesterol 178mg.

23. Zucchini Spinach Muffins

Preparation Time: 10 minutes | Cooking Time: 25 minutes | Servings: 4

Ingredients:

2 eggs

1/2 zucchini, grated

1/8 cup parmesan cheese, grated

1/4 cup feta cheese, crumbled

2 tbsp onion spring, chopped

1/4 cup coconut flour

1/8 cup butter, melted

2 tbsp parsley, chopped

1/4 tsp nutmeg

1/8 cup water

1/4 tsp baking powder

1/4 cup spinach, cooked

1/8 tsp black pepper

1/8 tsp salt

Directions:

In a bowl, whisk together eggs, water, butter, and salt.

Add baking soda and coconut flour and mix well.

Add onions, nutmeg, parsley, spinach, zucchini, parmesan cheese, feta cheese, pepper, and salt, and stir well.

Pour batter into the silicone muffin molds.

Place silicone muffin molds into the instant pot air fryer basket and place the basket in the pot.

Seal the pot with an air fryer lid and select bake mode and cook at 400ºF for 20-25 minutes.

Serve and enjoy.

Nutrition:

Calories 236, Fat 18g, Carbohydrates 4g, Sugar 1g, Protein 15g, Cholesterol 135mg.

24. Baked Coconut Chicken Wings

Preparation Time: 10 minutes | Cooking Time: 55 minutes | Servings: 4

Ingredients:

2 lbs chicken wings

1/8 tsp paprika

2 tsp seasoned salt

1/2 cup coconut flour

1/4 tsp garlic powder

1/2 tsp chili powder

Directions:

In a bowl, add all ingredients except chicken wings and

mix well.

Add chicken wings to the bowl and toss until well coated.

Line instant pot air fryer basket with parchment paper or foil.

Add chicken wings into the air fryer basket and place the basket in the pot.

Seal the pot with an air fryer lid and select bake mode and cook at 400°F for 55 minutes.

Serve and enjoy.

Nutrition:

Calories 440, Fat 17g, Carbohydrates 1g, Sugar 0.2g, Protein 66g, Cholesterol 202mg.

25.   **Butter Garlic Chicken**

Preparation Time: 10 minutes | Cooking Time: 40 minutes | Servings: 4

Ingredients:

2 lbs chicken drumsticks

1 fresh lemon juice

8 garlic cloves, minced

2 tbsp olive oil

4 tbsp butter, melted

2 tbsp parsley, chopped

Pepper

Salt

Directions:

Line instant pot air fryer basket with parchment paper or foil.

Add chicken into the large bowl and pour remaining ingredients over chicken and toss well.

Transfer chicken into the air fryer basket and place basket in the pot.

Seal the pot with an air fryer lid and select bake mode and cook at 400ºF for 35-40 minutes.

Serve and enjoy.

Nutrition:

Calories 560, Fat 31g, Carbohydrates 3g, Sugar 0.4g, Protein 62g,

26. Crunchy Pecan Crust Chicken

Preparation Time: 10 minutes | Cooking Time: 12 minutes | Servings: 4

Ingredients:

1 lb chicken tenders

1 cup pecans, crushed

2 tbsp maple syrup

1/4 cup ground mustard

1/2 tsp paprika

Pepper Salt

Directions:

Season chicken tenders with paprika, pepper, and salt.

Add maple syrup and mustard into the small bowl and mix well.

In a shallow dish, add crushed pecans.

Place the dehydrating tray in a multi-level air fryer basket and place basket in the instant pot.

Brush chicken tenders with maple syrup and coat with crushed pecans and place on dehydrating tray.

Seal pot with air fryer lid and select air fry mode then set the temperature to 350°F and timer for 12 minutes.

Serve and enjoy.

Nutrition:

Calories 281, Fat 14.2g, Carbohydrates 0.7g, Sugar 0g, Protein 33g, Cholesterol 116mg.

27. Brazilian Chicken Drumsticks

Preparation Time: 10 minutes | Cooking Time: 20 minutes | Servings: 4

Ingredients:

1 lb chicken drumsticks

1 tbsp olive oil

1/4 cup lime juice

1/2 tsp cayenne

1/2 tsp coriander seeds, crushed

1/2 tsp black peppercorns, crushed

1 tsp turmeric

1 tsp dried parsley

1 tsp dried oregano

1 tsp cumin seeds

1 tsp salt

Directions:

Add chicken drumsticks into the mixing bowl. Add remaining ingredients over chicken and coat well. Place in refrigerator overnight.

Spray instant pot multi-level air fryer basket with cooking spray.

Add marinated chicken drumsticks into the air fryer basket and place the basket into the instant pot.

Seal pot with air fryer lid and select air fry mode then set the temperature to 390°F and timer for 20 minutes.

Turn chicken halfway through.

Serve and enjoy.

Nutrition:

Calories 281, Fat 14.2g, Carbohydrates 0.7g, Sugar 0g,

Protein 33g, Cholesterol 116mg.

Chapter 3: Dinner Recipes

28. Low-Carb Meatloaf

Preparation Time: 10 minutes | Cooking Time: 20 minutes | Servings: 4

Ingredients:

1 egg

1 lb ground beef

1 tbsp garlic powder

1 tsp onion powder

1 1/2 tbsp Worcestershire sauce

2 tbsp tomato paste

1/4 cup half and half

1/4 cup almond flour

Pepper

Salt

Directions:

Spray a loaf pan with cooking spray and set aside.

Add all ingredients into the mixing bowl and mix until

well combined.

Transfer meat mixture into the prepared loaf pan.

Place steam rack into the instant pot then places loaf pan on top of the rack.

Seal pot with air fryer lid and select bake mode then set the temperature to 350°F and timer for 20 minutes.

Serve and enjoy.

Nutrition:

Calories 309, Fat 13.3g, Carbohydrates 6.9g, Sugar 2.9g, Protein 38.5g, Cholesterol 148mg.

29. Indian Meatloaf

Preparation Time: 10 minutes | Cooking Time: 15 minutes | Servings: 4

Ingredients:

2 eggs

1 lb ground beef

1/8 tsp ground cardamom

1/2 tsp ground cinnamon

1 tsp cayenne

1 tsp turmeric

2 tsp garam masala

1 tbsp garlic, minced

1/2 tbsp ginger, minced

1/4 cup fresh cilantro, chopped

1 cup onion, minced

Pepper

Salt

Directions:

Spray a loaf pan with cooking spray and set aside.

Add all ingredients into the mixing bowl and mix until well combined.

Transfer meat mixture into the prepared loaf pan.

Place steam rack into the instant pot then places loaf pan on top of the rack.

Seal pot with air fryer lid and select air fry mode then set the temperature to 360ºF and timer for 15 minutes.

Serve and enjoy.

Nutrition:

Calories 264, Fat 9.5g, Carbohydrates 5g, Sugar 1.5g, Protein 37.8g, Cholesterol 183mg.

30. Delicious Kababs

Preparation Time: 10 minutes | Cooking Time: 15 minutes | Servings: 4

Ingredients:

1 lb ground beef 1/4 tsp ground cinnamon

1/4 tsp ground cardamom 1/2 tsp cayenne

1/2 tsp turmeric 1 tbsp ginger, minced

1 tbsp garlic, minced 1/4 cup cilantro, chopped

1/4 cup mint, chopped 1/2 cup onion, minced 1 tsp salt

Directions:

Add meat and remaining ingredients into the mixing bowl and mix until well combined.

Place the dehydrating tray in a multi-level air fryer basket and place basket in the instant pot.

Make kababs into sausage shapes and place them on a dehydrating tray.

Seal pot with air fryer lid and select bake mode then set the temperature to 350ºF and timer for 15 minutes.

Turn kababs halfway through.

Serve and enjoy.

Nutrition:

Calories 229, Fat 7.3g, Carbohydrates 4g, Sugar 0.7g, Protein 35.1g, Cholesterol 101mg.

31. Trout and Radishes

Preparation time: 5 minutes | Cooking Time: 12 minutes | Servings: 4

Ingredients:

4 trout fillets, boneless and skinless

A pinch of salt and black pepper

1 tablespoon parsley, chopped

2 tablespoons tomato passata

2 cups red radishes, sliced

Directions:

In your instant pot, combine all the ingredients, put the lid on, and cook on High for 12 minutes.

Release the pressure fast for 5 minutes.

Divide everything between plates and serve.

Nutrition:

Calories 129, fat 5.3g, fiber 1.1g, carbs 2.5g, protein 17g.

32. Cod and Broccoli

Preparation time: 5 minutes | Cooking Time: 15 minutes | Servings: 4

Ingredients:

4 cod fillets, boneless and skinless

A pinch of salt and black pepper

1-pound broccoli florets

2 tablespoon tomato passata

1 cup chicken stock

1 tablespoon cilantro, chopped

Directions:

In your instant pot, combine all the ingredients, put the

lid on, and cook on High for 15 minutes.

Release the pressure fast for 5 minutes, divide the mix between plates and serve.

Nutrition:

Calories 197, fat 10g, fiber 3.1g, carbs 4.3g, protein 19.4g.

33.   Rosemary Trout and Cauliflower

Preparation time: 10 minutes | Cooking Time: 15 minutes | Servings: 4

Ingredients:

4 trout fillets, boneless and skinless

½ cup veggie stock

2 garlic cloves, minced

2 cups cauliflower florets

1 tablespoon avocado oil

A pinch of salt and black pepper

1 tablespoon rosemary, chopped

Directions:

Set the instant pot on Sauté mode, add the oil, heat it,

add the garlic and sauté for 2 minutes.

Add the rest of the ingredients, put the lid on, and cook

on High for 13 minutes.

Release the pressure naturally for 10 minutes, divide

the mix between plates and serve.

Nutrition:

Calories 140, fat 5.9g, fiber 1.8g, carbs 3.9g, protein

17.7g.

34. Cinnamon Cod Mix

Preparation time: 5 minutes | Cooking Time: 12 minutes | Servings: 4

Ingredients:

4 cod fillets, boneless and skinless

1 tablespoon cinnamon powder

1 cup cherry tomatoes, cubed

Juice of ½ lemon

½ cup veggie stock

A pinch of salt and black pepper

1 tablespoon cilantro, chopped

Directions:

In your instant pot, mix the fish with the rest of the ingredients, put the lid on and cook on High for 12 minutes.

Release the pressure fast for 5 minutes, divide everything between plates and serve.

Nutrition:

Calories 162, fat 9.6g, fiber 0.3g, carbs 3g, protein 16.5g.

35.   Trout and Eggplant Mix

Preparation time: 10 minutes | Cooking Time: 15 minutes | Servings: 4

Ingredients:

4 trout fillets, boneless

2 scallions, chopped

2 eggplants, cubed

½ cup chicken stock

2 tablespoons parsley, chopped

3 tablespoons olive oil

A pinch of salt and black pepper

2 tablespoons smoked paprika

Directions:

Set the instant pot on Sauté mode, add the oil, heat it, add the scallions and the eggplant and cook for 2 minutes,

Add the rest of the ingredients except the parsley, put the lid on, and cook on High for 13 minutes.

Release the pressure naturally for 10 minutes, divide the mix between plates and serve with the parsley sprinkled on top.

Nutrition:

Calories 291, fat 16.8g, fiber 4.5g, carbs 6.4g, protein 20g.

36. Salmon and Tomato Passata

Preparation time: 10 minutes | Cooking Time: 15 minutes | Servings: 4

Ingredients:

1 tablespoon olive oil

4 salmon fillets, boneless, skinless, and cubed

1 tablespoon rosemary, chopped

1 shallot, chopped

1 cup tomato passata

1 teaspoon chili powder

1 tablespoon chives, chopped

A pinch of salt and black pepper

Directions:

Set the instant pot on Sauté mode, add the oil, heat it, add the shallot and sauté for 2 minutes.

Add the rest of the ingredients, put the lid on, and cook on High for 12 minutes.

Release the pressure naturally for 10 minutes, divide the mix between plates and serve.

Nutrition:

Calories 291, fat 16.8g, fiber 4.5g, carbs 7.4g, protein 20g.

37. Salmon and Artichokes

Preparation time: 10 minutes | Cooking Time: 15 minutes | Servings: 4

Ingredients:

1-pound salmon, skinless, boneless, and cubed

2 spring onions, chopped

12 ounces canned artichokes, roughly chopped

1 and ½ cups chicken stock

A pinch of salt and black pepper

1 tablespoon cilantro, chopped

Directions:

In your instant pot, combine all the ingredients, put the lid on, and cook on High for 15 minutes.

Release the pressure naturally for 10 minutes, divide everything between plates and serve.

Nutrition:

Calories 193, fat 7.1g, fiber 4.1g, carbs 6.4g, protein 24.5g.

38. Trout and Spinach Mix

Preparation time: 5 minutes | Cooking Time: 15 minutes | Servings: 4

Ingredients:

6 trout fillets, boneless

2 tablespoons avocado oil

2 scallions, minced

2 garlic cloves, minced

2 tablespoons cilantro, chopped

1 cup baby spinach

A pinch of salt and black pepper

2 tablespoons balsamic vinegar

Directions:

Set the instant pot on Sauté mode, add the oil, heat it,

add the scallions and the garlic and sauté for 2 minutes.

Add the rest of the ingredients, put the lid on, and cook

on High for 12 minutes.

Release the pressure fast for 5 minutes, divide the mix

between plates and serve.

Nutrition:

Calories 194, fat 8.8g, fiber 0.7g, carbs 1.8g, protein

25.4g.

39. Sea Bass and Sauce

Preparation time: 10 minutes | Cooking Time: 15 minutes | Servings: 4

Ingredients:

4 sea bass fillets, boneless and skinless

2 tablespoons lime juice

2 garlic cloves, minced

1 shallot, chopped

1 cup chicken stock

1 cup tomato passata

A pinch of salt and black pepper

Directions:

In your instant pot, combine the fish with the rest of the ingredients, put the lid on, and cook on High for 15 minutes.

Release the pressure naturally for 10 minutes, divide the mix between plates and serve.

Nutrition:

Calories 154, fat 2.9g, fiber 1.3g, carbs 2.5g, protein 25g.

40. Sea Bass and Pesto

Preparation time: 5 minutes | Cooking Time: 12 minutes | Servings: 4

Ingredients:

4 sea bass fillets, skinless, boneless

2 tablespoons olive oil

2 tablespoons garlic, chopped

1 cup basil, chopped

2 tablespoons pine nuts

A pinch of salt and black pepper

1 cup tomato passata

1 tablespoon parsley, chopped

Directions:

In your blender, combine the oil with the garlic, basil, pine nuts, salt, and pepper and pulse well.

In your instant pot, combine the sea bass with the pesto, salt, pepper, tomato passata, and parsley, put the lid on, and cook on High for 12 minutes.

Release the pressure fast for 5 minutes, divide the mix between plates and serve.

Nutrition:

Calories 237, fat 12.7g, fiber 1.3g, carbs 5.5g, protein 25.8g.

Chapter 4: Snacks, Appetizers, And

Desserts

41. Easy Homemade French Fries

Preparation Time: 10 minutes | Cooking Time: 15

minutes | Servings: 4

Ingredients:

2 potatoes, peel & cut into fries' shape

1/2 tsp garlic powder

1/2 tbsp olive oil

Pepper

Salt

Directions:

Soak potato fries in water for 15 minutes. Drain well and

pat dry with a paper towel.

Toss potato fries with oil, garlic powder, pepper, and

salt.

Add potato fries to an instant pot air fryer basket and

place basket in the instant pot.

Seal pot with air fryer lid and select bake mode then set the temperature to 375ºF and timer for 10 minutes.

Turn fries to the other side and bake for 5 minutes more.

Serve and enjoy.

Nutrition:

Calories 90, Fat 1.9g, Carbohydrates 17g, Sugar 1.3g, Protein 1.9g, Cholesterol 0mg.

42.   Spicy Cashew Nuts

Preparation Time: 10 minutes | Cooking Time: 5 minutes | Servings: 6

Ingredients:

3 cups cashews

2 tbsp olive oil

1 tsp ground cumin

1 tsp ground coriander

1 tsp paprika 1 tsp salt

Directions:

Add cashews and remaining ingredients into the mixing bowl and toss well.

Place the dehydrating tray in a multi-level air fryer

basket and place basket in the instant pot.

Spread cashews on a dehydrating tray.

Seal pot with air fryer lid and select air fry mode then

set the temperature to 330ºF and timer for 5 minutes.

Serve and enjoy.

Nutrition:

Calories 436, Fat 36.6g, Carbohydrates 22.7g, Sugar 3.5g,

Protein 10.6g, Cholesterol 0mg.

43. Cinnamon Maple Chickpeas

Preparation Time: 10 minutes | Cooking Time: 12 minutes | Servings: 4

Ingredients:

14 oz can chickpeas, rinsed, drained and pat dry

1 tsp ground cinnamon

1 tbsp brown sugar

1 tbsp maple syrup

1 tbsp olive oil Pepper Salt

Directions:

Place the dehydrating tray in a multi-level air fryer basket and place basket in the instant pot.

Spread chickpeas on a dehydrating tray.

Seal pot with air fryer lid and select air fry mode then set the temperature to 375ºF and timer for 12 minutes.

Stir halfway through.

In a mixing bowl, mix cinnamon, brown sugar, maple syrup, oil, pepper, and salt. Add chickpeas and toss well to coat.

Serve and enjoy.

Nutrition:

Calories 171, Fat 4.7g, Carbohydrates 28.5g, Sugar 5.2g, Protein 4.9g, Cholesterol 0mg.

44. Parmesan Carrot Fries

Preparation Time: 10 minutes | Cooking Time: 15 minutes | Servings: 4

Ingredients:

4 carrots, peeled and cut into fries

2 tbsp parmesan cheese, grated

1 1/2 tbsp garlic, minced

2 tbsp olive oil

Pepper Salt

Directions:

Add carrots and remaining ingredients into the mixing bowl and toss well.

Spray instant pot multi-level air fryer basket with cooking spray.

Add carrots fries into the air fryer basket and place basket into the instant pot.

Seal pot with air fryer lid and select air fry mode then set the temperature to 350°F and timer for 15 minutes.

Stir halfway through.

Serve and enjoy.

Nutrition:

Calories 99, Fat 7.6g, Carbohydrates 7.2g, Sugar 3g, Protein 1.6g, Cholesterol 2mg.

45. Tater Tots

Preparation Time: 10 minutes | Cooking Time: 10 minutes | Servings: 2

Ingredients:

16 oz frozen tater tots

1 tbsp olive oil

Salt

Directions:

Drizzle tater tots with olive oil and season with salt.

Spray instant pot multi-level air fryer basket with cooking spray.

Add tater tots into the air fryer basket and place basket into the instant pot.

Seal pot with air fryer lid and select air fry mode then set the temperature to 400ºF and timer for 10 minutes.

Stir halfway through.

Serve and enjoy.

Nutrition:

Calories 492, Fat 28.6g, Carbs 54g, Sugar 1.4g, Protein 5.4g, Cholesterol 0mg.

46. Chili Lime Chickpeas

Preparation Time: 10 minutes | Cooking Time: 12 minutes | Servings: 4

Ingredients:

14 oz can chickpeas, rinsed, drained and pat dry

1 tbsp lime juice

1/4 tsp red pepper

1/2 tsp chili powder

1 tbsp olive oil Pepper Salt

Directions:

Add chickpeas, red pepper, chili powder, oil, pepper, and salt into the mixing bowl and toss well.

Place the dehydrating tray in a multi-level air fryer basket and place basket in the instant pot.

Spread chickpeas on a dehydrating tray.

Seal pot with air fryer lid and select air fry mode then set the temperature to 375ºF and timer for 12 minutes.

Stir halfway through.

Drizzle lemon juice over chickpeas and serve.

Nutrition:

Calories 154, Fat 4.7g, Carbohydrates 24.1g, Sugar 0.6g, Protein 5.1g, Cholesterol 0mg.

47. Strawberry Tart

Preparation time: 25 minutes | Cooking Time: 40 minutes | Servings: 8

Ingredients:

1 ½ cups almond flour

1/3 cup butter; melted

2 cups strawberries; sliced

5 egg whites

1/3 cup swerve

Zest of 1 lemon, grated

1 tsp. Baking powder

1 tsp. Vanilla extract

Cooking spray

Directions:

In a bowl, whisk egg whites well.

Add the rest of the ingredients except the cooking spray

gradually and whisk everything.

Grease a tart pan with the cooking spray and pour the

strawberries mix

Put the pan in the air fryer and cook at 370°f for 20

minutes.

Cool down, slice, and serve

Nutrition:

Calories 182, Fat 12g, Fiber 1g, Carbs 6g, Protein 5g.

48. Moroccan-Style Couscous Salad

Preparation time:10 minutes | Cooking Time: 10

minutes Servings 4

Ingredients:

1-pound couscous

1 tablespoon olive oil

2 tablespoons sesame butter tahini

2 tablespoons fresh mint, roughly chopped

2 bell peppers, diced

1 cucumber, diced 2 cups vegetable broth

1/4 cup yogurt

1 tablespoon honey

2 tomatoes, sliced

A bunch of scallions, sliced

Directions:

Press the "Sauté" button and heat the oil; then, sauté the peppers until tender and aromatic. Stir in the couscous and vegetable broth.

Secure the lid. Choose the "Manual" mode and cook for 2 minutes at high pressure. Once cooking is complete, use a quick pressure release; carefully remove the lid.

Then, stir in the remaining ingredients; stir to combine well and enjoy!

Nutrition:

Calories 563, Fat 9.2g, Carbs 98g, Protein 19.6g, Sugars 7.3g.

49.   Short Ribs with Herbs and Molasses

Preparation time:1 hour 45 minutes | Cooking Time: 10

minutes Servings 8

Ingredients:

3 pounds short ribs 1 tablespoon lard

4 cloves of garlic 1 teaspoon cayenne pepper

2 tablespoons rice vinegar 2 tablespoons molasses

2 rosemary sprigs 2 thyme sprigs

1 cup beef bone broth 1/2 cup port wine

Sea salt and ground black pepper, to season

Directions:

Press the "Sauté" button and melt the lard. Once hot,

cook the short ribs for 4 to 5 minutes, turning them periodically to ensure even cooking.

Add the other ingredients.

Secure the lid. Choose the "Manual" mode and cook for 90 minutes at high pressure. Once cooking is complete, use a natural pressure release; carefully remove the lid. Afterward, place the short ribs under the broiler until the outside is crisp or about 10 minutes. Transfer the ribs to a platter and serve immediately.

Nutrition:

Calories 372, Fat 27.6g, Carbs 4.9g, Protein 25.7g, Sugars 3.4g.

50.   Popcorn with A Twist

Preparation time:10 minutes | Cooking Time: 10 minutes

Servings 4

Ingredients:

1/2 tablespoon ground cinnamon

1/2 cup popcorn kernels

1/4 cup icing sugar

2 tablespoons coconut oil

Directions:

Press the "Sauté" button and melt the coconut oil. Stir until it begins to simmer.

Stir in the popcorn kernels and cover. When the popping slows down, press the "Cancel" button.

Toss the freshly popped corn with icing sugar and cinnamon. Toss to evenly coat the popcorn and serve immediately.

Nutrition:

Calories 295, Fat 11.5g, Carbs 42.2g, Protein 6.3g, Sugars 6.6g.

Conclusion

Thank you for reading this cookbook. Inspired by local food culture, environment, geography, religion, and cultural activities, comfort foods have always been treasured by food lovers. Be it summer or winter, these easy-to-prepare recipes are ideal for any occasion.

You're cooking for the family reunion, club meeting, or Sunday supper. You want to make the meal an event, and you want friends and family to feel the love.

Every recipe in this collection fills that bill—and more. Here you have more than 600 mouthwatering, heartwarming, craving-killing recipes, including the favorites named above. We're sure that you'll love them; we've tried them all.

CPSIA information can be obtained
at www.ICGtesting.com
Printed in the USA
LVHW061825190621
690654LV00002B/285

9 781801 711029